be r

STORM

STORM

new poems by

Alan Sillitoe

W. H. Allen · London
A division of Howard & Wyndham Ltd
1974

© ALAN SILLITOE, 1974
THIS BOOK OR PARTS THEREOF MAY NOT BE
REPRODUCED WITHOUT PERMISSION IN WRITING.
PRINTED IN GREAT BRITAIN BY THE ANCHOR PRESS LTD,
TIPTREE, ESSEX,
FOR THE PUBLISHERS W. H. ALLEN & CO. LTD,
44 HILL STREET, LONDON WIX 8LB
BOUND AT TIPTREE BY WM. BRENDON & SON LTD.
ISBN 0 491 01772 3

Acknowledgements

The present volume consists of poems collected since my last book LOVE IN THE ENVIRONS OF VORONEZH in 1968.

Nearly half the poems here have been printed in the following magazines and newspapers: The New Yorker; Shenandoah; Vanderbilt Poetry Review; Southern Review, Australia; PEN Anthology of New Poems 1973–74; Wave; Outposts; Gambit; The Scotsman.

The poem *Somme*, with a drawing by Ralph Steadman, was printed by The Steam Press at Bernard Stone's Turret Bookshop, 1973.

Six poems were printed in a volume of the Rainbow Press, together with poems by Ruth Fainlight and Ted Hughes (1971).

A further eight of the poems were published as a separate book called *Barbarians and Other Poems*, by Turret Books, 1973.

Contents

Chain

The chain is weakest at its strongest point
The strong link by its heart helps weaker parts,
And so weak links grow tauter than they should.

Thus, taking too much strength
The whole chain falls apart
Broken at both weak and stronger point.

Water breaks the strongest chain
When a storm-tide drags the ship away.
Power changes confidence—

The strongest link a strand of hair—
Weakest at its strongest point
That shares its heart with weaker hearts.

Love

What is love? You've heard it all before:
Everyone has: wounds that never heal
Scars corrupted by their own pain:
A mordant ache that will not go away—
A flying up the cataract of death.

First love is the first door to it.
There are many more.
Unlock each one, you have no choice,
Or if you turn from it with despair
Because you see its end already,
Watch the unknown shove it down for you
And feel death draw you through it,
And into love again, again and yet again.

What can you do except go in,
Go through, even if you feel the scar
Before the wound begins to bite.
Love stays.
Its ecstasy is eaten by the wound.
The wound is avaricous and consumes your life.

What more do you want?

Hephzibah

Hephzibah is a beautiful name.
Why don't I use it when I write or speak?
I passed your window but no light was on.
I do not use the word 'love'
In vain nor easily. Not at this stage
Of the game. Its fuses
Smoke in the snows of the heart
Ignite the wind, glutton the marrow
As I watch the bombed space
Phosphorised to blindness, subsiding
Slowly. I am a different man. You
Cannot answer my letters
Or speeches. Salt is burning,
Burns till there is no more light.
Traffic signals change
In the palm of my hand
Before a gale wipes them finally out.
Machinery begins.
I don't forget your name or use it,
But continually hear those syllables
Shriller than the mad woman's curse
As she speeds through traffic
With white headlights flooding the road.

Naked

Naked, naked, I never see you naked
As if to be naked is to tell lies
With the body that you show—
Cover it against those lies.

Hide naked, keep it close
You never let me see you naked
Unless half so by accident or tease.
Hide it carefully : those lies are yours.
Speak them loudly if they burn. Yours,

Not mine. I see you naked through them
Through love, naked beyond the lies of nakedness
That will not let you see yourself

Naked. But keep yourself concealed and pure:
The lies that hide you are less sure
Than those that blind me.

I Love You

Juliet loved Mercutio whom Romeo slew
So she killed Romeo and then herself—
My version is as good as any
For love is the sweetest carnage
And love is dead
So long live love—
The window-pane a bloodshot
Eye that looks on it.
Horizons fall into my hands:
I let them through.

Take
L and strangle it
O and fuck it
V and pull it apart
E annihilate it
And wear it as a necklace
And with the I, black it,
Blind it, close it with tape and gum
Scoop it out and stamp on it with ice boots.
You can eat it shit it out
Pick it up with your hobble-gobble cunt
And conceive the world's great monstrous bastard
In the image of a misbegotten love
That I LOVE YOU and YOU LOVE ME that sank
        thank God
Into the bottomless sea:
Only a third eye cures a headache
The third eye seeing all the world
And right through you
The I LOVE YOU, the wasted tombstones

Of that graveyard fevergrate
And fragrant skyfart
Spelling YOU LOVE ME
They died together at eighty three
Bindweed ties a ghost ship to the quay
With rotting rope of smoke and stinkweed—

The seed I shot over foam and waves
Is free, for I DON'T LOVE
And never will because I can't, and seek
Horizons to break over my knee
And trees to eat
And dead fish to throw at the stars.

Lover's Plea

Those who want nothing
Know nothing,
So get me to promise something
Make an impossible demand.
Go on, ask me so that I may discover
How to break mine and your spell
Over this ruined love
That might keep us together.

To ask is to define—
Get me to promise that
Before you promise me—
A fantastic absolute request
Of definition as to what I mean and want
That only the love we might yet have
Can need or answer for.

So go on, ask me with a smile
Of ever-demanding victory
Something that you think
Could still keep us together,
So that I can finally
Say no.

Sea Talk

Talk on the beach:
Love has a broken heart
Is a pomegranate split
With a waterfall pouring in
To it. Each half lifts
Drifts out to sea
Eaten clean as January boats
By frost and salt:

One will sink, one survive:
Withered fruit-husk without salt
Or soul. It could be you, and could
Be me, watching January waves
Erupt like whales and thrones and tractors:
Stones clash back into familiar places.

You wait for a boat to come
And get you from this pandemonium
Of humping tide and screeching stones.
But what ship wrecked you there?
Want to know, and cease to wonder.
The boat lurches into seas of danger
Waves turning phosphorous, turn fire:
Rowers start to row, and you not with them
When the numbness in you burns
And you do not want to go
Or stay.

Pomegranate is a far-off fruit.
Scattered seeds fulfil no circle.

Love cannot kill
A broken heart, nor mend it;
The sea defends its dead
And those born from it,
Believes in broken hearts,
Burns when it boils so.
No boat can stay, must fall apart
Floating through the open heart,
Like fruit bursting
At the shock of moonless water
Back to these feet that cannot move,
And two more hearts pulled in to slaughter.

Last Thoughts

Love affair ended:
Put black on both elbows
And disinfect what warmth of heart is left
Smear the face in mummery-misery,
Show her the back of your head
Where the moon-boil burrows
Like a festering fire-tick.

She cannot guess, but only say
Leave me alone, speak to me,
Speak to me, leave me alone,
Or burn to spiritual death
In the white flames of indifference.
Rather that. Let that be.
Love affair ended.
Nothing is ended
If that is not ended.

Ghosts

It is time to part
Before murder is done.
We have robbed each other
Of all we ever had,
Scoffed grey mud of the battleground
(And packed our brains with it)
Digested the gall of blood and loot
So that we can't give it back
In that pure state it was before:
We have consumed ourselves
Without horror or disgust
In that ignoble life's work of love.

All that we can do
Is part like ghosts,
Promising not to haunt each other
Or make ghosts of others.

Goodbye Kursk

The thin moon
Sliced out the heart as it fell
Then effortlessly made its way
To the earth's true middle:
The only cure for jealousy
Is to fall in love again.
The moon gives back what it takes away.

Blocks of flats blot out the moon.
People live with happiness and work.
I left my love too soon, too soon.
Wait for me, and write to me:
It won't seem long.

She looked at me
Put sugar in my coffee
Filled my pipe
Shed tears when I left.
In my eyes
I felt the light of death.

It won't seem long,
Hull down, the tank waiting:
I see them coming through the dust.

Toasting

Drink, blackout, gutter-bout
Kick back nine swills of vodka
That put an iron band around
Thorned skullcap and fire
Of sulphurous words toasting
Life, peace, town or cousin.

Bottles, heaped grub, dead towers in tabletown :
Wine descends in light and colour
As if the Devil had a straw stuck there
Greedily drawing liquid in
As my consciousness draws out.

W

Poets are vampires
Greedy, vain and vicious.
Don't ask me how I know it.
I just do—

Looking at Cassiopeia in the sky
That vast lit-up interrogative about to swoop
Which sets me wondering:

When will it be?
Who?
What for?
And, in any case,
Why?

Railway Station

Death is the apotheosis of the bourgeois ethic.
Tolstoy, when he felt it coming on
Left his family and set off towards Jerusalem.
No one said that he was psychopathic.

Death shared its railway station, with him
Who in a coma heard trains banging
Along that platform where Anna Karenin
Was violated in her greatest longing

Under the snake of crushing wheels.
The fourth bell drowned his final wrath.
The Bolsheviks renamed that station Tolstoy—
Instead of Bourgeois Death.

Open Plan

Homilies for families:
Advice-card on colours.

Catonic pinks/
Stainless-steel sinks.

Paranoid blues/
Blocked-up flues.

Catalepsy yellows/
Soft feather pillows.

Schizoid browns/
All day in dressing gowns.

Neurotic reds/
Extra wide beds.

Household paints
For Newly-weds.

Full Moon's Tongue

She said, when the full moon's tongue hung out
Over the Earls Court chimney pots,
And he circled forever (slowly)
Round the square to find
A suitable parking place—

She said: Take me away: let's go together.

Keep clear, he said. You'd better not.
I'll take you, but watch out,
For I will bring you back, he said,
If at all,
In two pieces.

She said: I'll never want to come back
If I go away with you.

They all do, he said.
I'll bring you back in two pieces
And you'll live like that
Forever
And never join them up again.

How cruel, she said, seeing what he meant.

O no, he said. To take you apart completely
From yourself and make two separate pieces
Might be the one sure way of fixing
A whole person out of you—
If that's what you want.
Some do, some don't.
He was exceptionally nonchalant.

I'm not sure now, she said,
Screaming suddenly : You bastard.
Let me get out.
I want to walk.

He stopped the car
But could not park it,
Someone behind with maybe a similar problem
Was hooting him to move,
So she jumped free and walked away
Leaving him bewildered
And in at least two pieces.

You talk too much,
Said one piece to another.

Who Died of Love?

Who died of love?
I did, said Balashov.
It stuck in my throat
And choked me to death.
My veins flowed with amber
My penis was granite.
I died of love—
So I walk very fast.

Love scraped off my hair
And blunted my teeth.
The sky gets a smile
When I think to look up.
I died of love,
So my lungs play shy
When the wind blows hot
And the wind blows cold
Just like her breath.

I drove my stake
Right through her heart.
It burst;
A red umbrella
A purple mushroom
A green tree—
I sit under each in turn
Blinking at the sun
And swallowing her rain.

Lovers

He stood looking at the sea.
She stood looking at the ocean.
They stood and looked at the same water.

He saw animal tails hanging from the sky
Serpent-tips lashing the wet lid of the flood.
Drum noise blocked his ears
But Heaven did not scare him.

She saw mountains piercing the top of the world:
A snowfall sweep into the pushing sea
Where it melted and was buried.
Under the surface it was red
But Hell did not frighten her.

They did not talk or hold hands
At the huge tide coming in:
His grandfather was a blacksmith,
And hers a cantor in the synagogue.

Plague-Meeting

At this party all the lights are low
An alcoholic scythe cuts down the shoots of reason.
Music cauterizes,
And blood burns all feeling from its own veins.

When the blinds are down and London burns
When cars through darkness
Bleed the street lights blue behind;
When music comes in cans and bottles
And spills against some long skirt
Or pair of trousers so that stains never come out;
When music is a powder on the tongue
That can't be swallowed—
Do I live?

Gorgeous women talk their powderous words
And see each others tinder eyes take fire—
De-odorous they smile and dance
Do nothing till the party
Puts you back into yourself,
When the last black ligament is chopped
And you float away from some shore
(Where butter-hamlets and prawn-girls
Linger, unchanging church-spires
Chip God's unchanging sky; where
Fishmen and plow-women smile on that cheese
        wrapper)
I drift towards land's end of real
Where the midnight lighthouse is on fire
With fireships running across the sea to put it out,
I do more than nothing and take someone to kiss—

Eel-pie and ringlets, small breasts
And fagteeth, a real beauty in this unreal land—
Who burns me into nothing as we kiss.
I feel her land in my mouth
Burning me, a train travelling,
A subterranean cave-in scorching
(I say to her)
Your incense and my impotence.

We are old lovers who've just met:
Your beauty, my youth; my orgy, your orgasm;
My lies, your languishing; my love, your
Visitation; my rage, your hunger; my
Nothing else except love, your need to make
Me need you when I always did
But couldn't when I met you—my
Visitation in this room where we can love
Alone and yet do nothing.

Burn down this party—they are not real
Not as your words and my false reassurances—
One can meet here but not love
Remember it and start to wait
Float on the straits between those butter-shores
And drown before the land of love can draw us out.
I can do nothing, so kiss the tits of dawn
And wait for the cancerous day,
Walk down the empty road and hear birds
In every tree.

Situation

You are where you are
Where your feet touch ground
Part of the soil that your shoes press down
On the long kiss of pavement or field
You are nowhere else
Neither in old age nor childhood
But only in now at this minute
On this actual part of the earth.

Even what you see does not alter it
Only reinforces where you are
And tells you you are here
Exactly where you are
And nowhere else
Where your head touches sky
And your eyes in looking upwards
Fix the clouds with their stare
But only briefly
Because the feet that hold you
Give the longest touch of earth
Telling you where you are—
Before taking you to where you go
And drawing me to where you are
And drawing you to where I am.

Place without a Name

(song for the ragman's daughter)

Where's that other country
With a street like this—
Where we'd feel the same way,
Be in love, yet free?

If only I could live there
And still be me
Meeting you
Only you—

I would like to live where
Everybody's free
Where we'd feel the same way—
What is that place called?

I would like to go there
And live—with you
In that Place
That's got no name.

Spanish New Year

I gulp each bitter grape
From the half-filled dish of water,
Witnessing the dragon-like old year die
With glittering scabs for each gone day
Holding tight their poison
Of decay and treachery.

The months spread evenly
On each moonface
An acid spittle pulsing at the tail
To burn at the last midnight minute
As I try to stop it
Shambling back into the bygone year.
My Jack o' Lantern head spits fire.

Between the strokes of one and twelve
I see how many grapes will go;
A stomach fills but does not fatten
When one is fighting with that dragon,
Whose coal-eye stirs and winks
And shows the way I will not follow.

Its last igniting farewell power
Split an ulcer in my brain
Which cascades up into a great new firework
        year;
He got me, I thought, killed me again,
As I vomit the old year out
Watch him eat it up and choke on it.

View from Misk Hill

The armies have already met, and gone.
When the best has happened, the worst is yet to come.
When the worst vanishes, beware of its return.
In summer the fields are grey and should be green.
The scars are rubbed with ash and sulphur.
At night the full moon clears the sky for its own view,
And if the moon had fangs it would favour this field
With neither roots nor hayricks, sheep nor stubble.
Whoever can may walk between the dried-up ulcers.

The evening is quiet. Birds are flying
Where the hills are green
And armies are not fighting yet.
From the ashpits of now he looks a long way onward,
Then walks between more craters, crossing
Fields with neither ditch nor hedge.

Where the land dips it is green, and smells of life.
Topography is wide down there, lit bright
By the moon for him: it smells of fire.
There are fields enriched for the harvest
Birds fattening before migration,
Smoke of the last summer between earth and sky
Youth and growing-up—
Land where armies have not yet thought to meet
But will, as he passes through.

February Poems

I.

Forests can become a desert,
The soul may die and turn to ash:
But will the sand send out new blossoms
Let flowers and trees grow strong again?

Do not be afraid of deserts:
There's a forest in each grain of sand—
The nearest to a sea on land
That breaks the eyes that look at it,

Making blind who want to see
More clearly after the disaster
Of losing memory and sight,
Till blindness in its vision sees
More boundaries than life and death.

In the desert that was once a forest
Opened eyes mean dust and thirst:
Tears dry up before one drinks them
Or any blood that freely flows.

Sand grains fly up nostrils
To cool off in protecting flesh,
Salting the blood as you enrich the desert—
Perishing in action.

There is a brittle plant whose seed
Drops of blood can reach and feed:
In the middle of the deepest sand-grain
A jewelled waterdrop creates new life.

But only blood, the spent and sweated marrow of
      despair
Can give such sustenance,
So search it out and get new life,
Make a forest from the driest desert.

II.

Hope is a message to the grave,
A built-in longing for the end
For something new—
Smelling soil and following the wind
Unravels any distance.

Hope cannot be forgiven its trickery,
Of crushing the black beetle of the past
And denying present terrors absolutely.

When hope takes hold, its ruthlessness
Feeds on the purest fuel of injustice
And sharpens the spike for action.

III.

Whatever you want—you cannot get:
Be careful what you want, in case you get it;
That chill river of desire flowing through the
      stomach
Surges on and on.

The only thing is to be
Glad it drives through you
And separates the borders of your body.

Do not be unhappy at its touch
But suffer as it goes
Letting resolution run with it.

The lime and ice it leaves you with
Contains the sediment of what you want,
And when you turn to get it
Icy banks will break
And change the river's course.

IV.

Let go, fall,
Feet ripping through snow-ladders
Losing field-views
And dunes of pepper beyond
Ampersand-trees stuck in
The withered arm of the horizon.
Between the toll of lazar-bell
Calling the snow-sick into hole
And hiding, the yellow eye
Of winter's snake-sun
Pushes a needlebeam into the heart
And paralyses it.

Open the hands, and let go.

V.

When love's game is ended
Life can begin again.
Start to live and you begin to die.
The game robs you of life.

After a week of rain
A hill slides towards the house
Bringing a smell of spring and mud
That freshens the brain. Red-ochre
And water slop at the bank
As I wade through it. Our game
Is never ended while blood wakens with the
        flowers.

He did not die,
But found a ladder
The last rung before death
And earth's last drop
Into the blackness of its fire.

The house is an island,
A mudtrack to the paved road washed
By flooding after months of drought.
No black sky can finish off that game,
Or engines drown the memory of peace.

VI.

February. I've seen you forty times
Already. Snow, rain, mud—

Tunnels going through each seam
A sky-arrow towards spring.
Some februaries face both ways,
A pivot turning on the heart
And showing the desert in which
Toni Moreno perished long ago.

But all those februaries are not left behind :
Forty swirling fish will never vanish.
Some are colourless, others like rainbows,
Twisted after strange journies,
Showing faces like moons and flanks like houses.
Each one paralyses whole aquariums.

February is creation,
The end of a ten-year funnel,
Thrust of unseen lives
The month I wait for to say goodbye to
February-earth and soaking loam
A zodiac that hexes me
One month when I watch the earth
And say a loud goodbye of welcome to.

VII.

Through a gap in snowlace curtains
I left the winter swamp for fire and sun,
Fell into the white and jewelled snake-eye
Of the universal serpent

Such heat shrivels heart and liver
Into rotten walnuts, makes the earth

A board to spread out on
While burning.

          Bless the earth:
The dust is yours, drummed solid
By that white sun coming down—
A fire of needle-tips tattoo white
Cat-scars on the sky surrounding it.

It burns and there is no escape
From the flat white iron of the sun.
Don't be afraid: lie flat as parchment.
No one can know
What its drumbeats tattoo on the brain.

There is no living fauna left
But serpent-skeletons
Bleached so clean the weakest breath
Can blow away such bones—
If any corpse can reach it.
The white hot circle of the sun
Can black out life,
But the earth is yours:
Lie flat, bless it, stroke the dust,
Before rain comes and rivers overflow.

VIII.

Be free, and suffer happiness—
Be happy in suffering.
Summer may come like a black dream from the
     grave
To mark your heart.

Winter can be a season of eternal joy
That prints a flower on your forehead.
The elegiac falling of the snow
Will make the purest blossoms grow.
The gentle warmth of green-eyed August
Spreads the odour of a wheatfield's death.

We do not know
What the sky-breath whispers at midday.
Choices bite whichever one performs
On the stage of your white hand.
Seed scattered over bitter loam
Can bring up crops and colours
That rub out happiness
Or August or suffering.

IX.

Mimosa dead after sixteen years yellowing life
And a smell that followed everywhere
Of unhappiness and death. Mimosa
Has the most treacherous stench of all the flowers.

Eucalyptus bark hanging like strips of flesh
From the unkillable body-tree
Is never consumed by the sun
Or swilled away by rain
But rots, in time, like human bodies
And the hearts that go with them.

The compost of eucalyptus and mimosa
Takes a long time to decompose
And send new flowers.

41

X

Midnight comes at any hour—
Eagles out of sunlight bring it
Wings that hide the day
And cover fields with shadow-moss.

The sun is fighting with black midnight
Throwing broken eagles
Back against the stars.
The moon eats them and grows fat.

The curtain goes up on a blue and empty sky.

Le Tholonet
1967–1968

Silence and Stillness

Silence and stillness
Are most prized in a whirlwind.
To be mad is to be caught
Between the millstones of stillness
To feel the body-bones
Living out the agony of the heart.

The whirlwind tries to penetrate the eyes,
The stockade of a gaze erected
So unseeing
That nothing can break through it
As you look and wait for the world
To act and pull you from it,
Into the body of someone
Who will draw all pain away.

A lawn grows in the palm of one hand:
Trees in the other combust
And smash into the lawn
To chase out worms.
What can soothe the battered soul?
Love cauterizes madness.

The Weight of Summer

The iron of summer is on the trees,
A new weight,
Leap-year sap rising through lead,
Forcing blossom and flower to give fruit,
Green flame of sap shifting up iron trunks
To poke out buds and leaves
And shelter the house from wider views.

Leaves hang all summer
Shaken by rain and wind
Shrived by a little heat
Caught between a thick roof and the ground.

This yearly swing must wear them
To a death so flat by autumn
That blood draws back
And lets the leaves go.

Trees look battered in frost and snow
Force-fed by soil and drained by age
They now brood emptily and bide their time.
How many summers can they take such weight?
How long is life, how rich the earth,
How weak the heart?

Rose

A rose about to open
Thinks that air and sun
Can turn it into
Something it is not already.

The pink slit of life it shows
Between the tight green blades—
Hasn't it seen enough
Without wanting everything?

Behind its packed unopened petals
Are all the roses still to open
All the petals that have not yet dropped;
Outside, those same are tempting it,
Scorched and shrivelled on the grass.
Rose about to open, why do you do it?

What force behind it pushes
So subtly that it does not feel it?
What beckoning power beyond
Draws it with perfumes sweeter than
The one that will be made?
They promise nothing but the last decay:
The will to come or stay is not its own.

Hunger

I haven't found my hunger yet. When will I find
The hunger to eat these walls away?
The smallest creature visible to the human eye
Ran up this page
As if the pale blue lines on it did not exist
And when I crushed it, hungry at its freedom,
I found it was a tiny spider made of brick.
It had lived on brick, the bright red dust of brick
That filled its dust-dot of a body and even the speck
Of legs it ran upon. Its life was fed by dust,
The dust of bricks, and it had found its hunger
Out of its deep birth, slaked it by living easily
On life, with no questions asked or even thought of.
Eating through walls was its life, its vital hunger
For the walls it ate through, even at times
Without hunger. It was so far in front,
So superior to me that I turned
And crushed it, which left a reddish smear
On the page, and on me, to remind me
Of the hunger that I have not found
But know about at last.

Storm (at Bellagio)

Rip your silk and split planks:
That's how it sounds
At the beginning of a storm.
I hear everything but see nothing
Till your voice changes:
Flay the flanks of Lombardy,
Throw your wagons down the hill
And sink them like boulders in the lake.
Flash-lightning buries against livid foothills,
Blunts its teeth on villas
With pink shutters and grey walls,
Chases pigeons to the eaves.
A storm clears the air, settles everything.

I don't believe it. Storm is life, a war on peace,
Though it's useless to fight you. We sit
Inside our small house drinking tea.
Like fate, you are only defeated by a mute
Witnessing of terrors. Your uncouth bullying
Sends a flood to bless the earth,
Mother's milk to a baby.

For nearly a week you've stormed
At every house and stone, and we've
Had enough of your reverberating flat hand
Flailing the mirror of the lake
Into sudden white wave-flowers
That send boats scooting to their villages.
Your lightning winks across our window
Till the whole pane becomes a metal
Mouth greedy to eat up its own flash:

I am afraid to run between the big trees
And visit our friends in their house below:
Your rain is too much, flowing
Into the lake which does not need it anymore,
Gouging gullies in the hills as it goes down—

Fate: of you, of all sorts, I've had enough.
How much longer will you flash and bawl at me?
Reach for the flesh of my heart to block
The veins of it? You shout and threaten, and I listen
To your cannonading din, that quarry-blasting
In the brain of the sky, those spackling
Rocket trajectories passing between Switzerland and
      Italy,
Licking high peaks on their way while the white rain
Bleeds over the javelin-peninsula of Bellagio
On which the ice-age split itself in two,
That sharp schizoid tongue pointing in derision
At the whole of northern europe, and I say
Leave me alone. I've had enough.

The noise scares and bores into my bones.
I wonder what comes next: not of your black
Concatenating dirge but out of my flayed
Thundergut and hidden lightning-bowl
Of white rain and pale powder mixing
Under the internal burning of the blood—

The seven-league loudest smasher of them all
Turns me from such wheedling thought: the true veil
Of rain rushes down as if to heaven,
Which is no longer in the sky
But completely the other way—

I shake my fist and spit at you, lift my boot
At your noisy reminders, at your fate and my fate
That will destroy my heart only when it melts
At last into the soil. And then, while the sky
Still storms its way around the earth
The blood of me will lapse into silence.

Fox

Fox, lie still,
Stay flat, make
My stomach warm.
Your mouth guards
My liver, you curl
Up and circle my intestines,
Keeping the earth
Inside me warm
And teaching me to wait.

We were born together
Crying at the same
Ox-eyed star for light
And food, till I pushed
The soil from my eyes
Saw you and swallowed hard:
And you jumped in me
For a hiding place
To find the warmest
Den you knew.

You taught me to wait.
We guide each other
Through the swamp.
Stars have fallen into it.
We talk to each other.
Seeing me alone
People think I'm mad:
But I lie still like a fox
Waiting to spring at the moon
And pull it down
To burn us up with it.

Odours

I smell death
Its odour has wafted
Through the years
When I'm in love.

Strongest at birth
It stayed a long time
But finally went—
Yet coming back from time to time.

Now I smell love
Mixing in with it.
It comes and goes
One pulling the other
Each unmistakable
And intermixing.

I smell love, a holy odour
Wafted from the years ahead
Like death—
The blades of helicopters stir it up.

The Dead

The dead—only want to be forgotten.
Having passed that painted door
They do not want to be disturbed
By fumes or clamour from the earth they left
And feared for all their life to leave.
While they were afraid of it
They loved as much as they were able,
Drew close as lovers or lost brothers,
But once that terrifying limit had been passed
They wanted sleep in death—
As once they tried to rest in life.
They only wanted us to remember them when dead
Before they died, but now that they are dead
They want nothing more than not to know,
To forget the monstrous door that let them through.
Perhaps we need them still, but they—are dead.
The living want to be forgiven,
And hope their turn will never come.

Pilgrim

The bread is polluted.
Break it; smell it:
Cordite, aluminium shavings,
A dash of mercury—
Christ ate shit
But knew where it came from.
The circuit he made was not polluted
Except by himself.

Mares that drink at watermills go mad,
Turn their jaws towards the sky
As if to smash it.
The air continually breeds disease.
No machines can measure it.

The saint rots in his cave
And taps his prayers onto a stone
Grunting his last strength out
At the end of his chain.
Only his eyes can give advice—
A vacant blind roll-around
That smokes the heart
And makes it fit to burst.
So pass him by. Through
The rich sky of summer
A thunderstorm slowly paints its way
Whitely from the horizon.
I push it against the shoulder of the world.

My head is open to the sky:
A drop of water hits the bare brain

And dies like fat in the fire
As if the wind spat a coin of flame there
Leaving the embers duller than before—
Dull veins that drive me to polluted bread
And back again, and on,
And round, and on again—
Towards a sea that never ends.

The Fall

Snow rots the soul.
It lays over the soil
In a deep seam,
Unable to go down as water
And complete its journey.
It dries the skin to look at snow,
Makes my eyes burn and worry
At the spectrous whiteness
Of so many particles
Let go as raindrops by the sky.

Each one had such beauty in its fall.
Those that lit on fields lay waiting
To be let into the earth.
Others on roads are crushed
Like butterflies that die
Without protest as their souls
Flow away in the mudwater
Of salt and gravel, the lucky ones
That end their journey soonest.

In youth snow gave me energy.
These days I am afraid of it,
Watch guardedly at every grain
In case it forms a monster—
Taller than a house,
A wild mare to gallop forward like a wall
And bury me.

The first snow flakes stop on the hard earth,
Gently at the door waiting to be let in.

They are crushed and smothered
By those masses coming after
That cannot be counted
X-rayed or measured
Or warmed back to life without dying
    first.
Only the darkness keeps them safe.

I watched this silent one-way
Absent-minded insane falling of the
    snow
I wanted to walk in
And, waving my arms,
Tell each insect of snow to go back
Go back
Go back because this was not the way
No good would come of it
Either for earth or sky—
Looking each bleak and suicidal
Snowflake in its white eye
To din my message in
That they were doomed
And so were dooming everything;
Wanted to get them driving
Deep into my mouth and save
The soil its leprous covering,
Piss them out in future sun
On a scarecrow's garden.

They flew in my face
And melted at its sweat—
Stone-deaf and spat there by the wind.
I slammed the door
And closed each window,

Sat in my corner as they came down
In the dark, through
The ceiling, into all rooms,
Melting on me, and flooding the world.

Autumn

Autumn sharpens all sense
With the twin blades of coal and frost.
Fog in the street hides misty hollows:
Incense of fireworks and mud.
Bayrose and blackberries wilt
Where stinging-nettles weep and rot.

I dreamed Salt Peter walked
(Seawrack clinging to his lips)
Through the mist lit by a rosebay sun:
Jack Frost came in time to help him cure
The autumn pig
And puzzle out the year's hard lock.
They tilted up the winter mill
Churning snow which burned like sulphur.

Lamp posts glitter through fog:
Sulphur-torches on a road
That has no turning—
Except backwards.

II.

I laced up my autumn boots,
Put on a coat and stalked from lamp to lamp
Where darkness was lighter than the home
With shouts of my own people:
Stray dogs and bonfires flicker,
Cats flee along secret by-paths
Of curved teeth.

Frost painted my cheeks with marble cold
And my toes with luminous tips
In their hide-outs:
But none of us kids liked rain
Drizzling on moss and bricks,
Found the house more homely
For the shelter and the food we got—
Brothers and sisters going through
One door for warmth.

The cold ambushed us when we got to bed
All four between brass nobs and rails,
An attic to ourselves in a minute cottage
In the Valley of the Leen where Nottingham
Stopped on its outward march,
Fixed by the green fields.

Two in the middle were warmest:
Except for suffocation, bliss.
But those on the outside
One of whom was me
Slept with a grip of bedclothes
In their fists, a fight kept up
Throughout grey dreams of Jack Frost
And Salt Peter when
To let go or relax
Meant shivering the whole long dawn.

III.

That's winter.
But autumn led to it

And into spring which marched
Again to autumn. Time is a wheel
And I stand in the middle
Facing one way, the roundabout
That spins each season slowly in
And either warms my face or freezes it.

Time
Lives nowhere but in memory,
Keeps me warm against the frost
And cool from the sun's bleak fire.

Creation

God did not write:
He spoke.
He made.
His jack-knife had a superblade.
He sliced the earth
And carved the water,
Made man and woman
By an act of slaughter.

He scattered polished diamonds
In the sky—like dust—
And gave the world a push to set it spinning.
What super-deity got him beginning,
Whispered in his ear on how to do it
Gave hints on what was to be done?

Don't ask.
In his mouth he felt the sun
Spat it out because it burned;
From between his toes—the moon—
He could not walk so kicked it free.
His work was finished.
He put a river round his neck,
And vanished.

Lamp Post

Strong, once permanent, and twelve feet tall,
An obsolescent lamp post
Is about to be uprooted
By a block-and-tackle gibbet,
One of many planted on that street—
Whose incandescent memories
Are cool and out for good.

Fluted trunk and crosstrees high
Head uplifted and extinguished:
Once its sober glare lit tracks
For boozers weaving late from pubs:
A beanpole for mad cars to bump at—
A man once tried to stare it out:
Gas fed its flame. God turned it off.

A question-hook spins up
(Unfitted for the lamp post's view)
By a workman in his cabin
Sorting levers like a hangman,
Who holds the still full-vigoured beacon
Lopsided for a final look along the street:

Crashes out of sunlight, into lorry.

Signal Box

Level-crossing signal box at night:
With three and a half hours between trains.
Bells stopped, gates shut and blocking the line,
Levers taller than himself palisade the moon
With him on the safe side of it.

A fox below is baffled at the spent trail
Ending in steel,
Soft rain filling the black spring night
And fields around.
No traffic: the last green spitter of sparks

Has elbowed space aside and tunnelled
Up the stars and soaking turf towards London,
Whispered along, snarling, a retreating song,
Signals falling on gauges like slicked hair down-
        arrowed,
A white face astonished: line clear,
For the next open crossing.

Guard in waistcoat, and jacket,
Good to children who just want to see:
Power slips through his fingers a hundred times a
        day:
Warns others down the line of its approach,
Sits by his teaflask and prepares a book.

Responsibility too great to feel powerful
He needs an opium-portion to become
Captain of a rusting steamer
Crawling the coastal buffs of Patagonia;

Or a Nemo in his flying boat
Lording it at the Pole or South Sea hideout.
One book every night, he says, is better
Than the telly or a homely bed.

Trains growl and twist on steel snakes
Straight and sleeping close together,
Locomotive kings of the dawn
And lions of the night
Coming behind signals drilling in
To cure his dreams and incurable sleep:
The fox turns back beyond that other door.
Wide gates wait for the first black arrow,
Packed and moving, a violent circle in its forehead
        middle:
He leaves his book, opens all gates,
And lets the day pour through.

Barbarians

The walls he sat by had fallen long ago.
When the city smoked after capture and rape
No brick was left upon another.

These barbarians—this boy
Sitting on the still littered grass—
Belonged to a Scythian family.
They found the city as if following
A far-back shutter-flash in the brain,
Crazed with hope after a famished
Trudge over the steppe whose herbs
Scorched by the wicked haze of the sun
Pulled the horses ribs so far in
They were almost dead.
By tale and memory
This Scythian off-shoot saw
A city of goods and people
And laden horses queueing to get out.

The city was empty, no brick
Upon another while the boy's
Mother scraped between heaps
Of mortardust. He played
At tapping stone with stone, his cracked lips
Moving at the sky, not knowing what else to do.
He waited for her to bring food,
And idly placed one brick on another.

Somme

A trench-map from the Battle of the Somme
(It doesn't matter where I got it)
Has a dead fly still stuck
At the bottom left-hand corner,
By a place called Longueval,
Rusty from the red blood sucked
Out of British (or German) soldiers
Long since gone over the top
Or to Tipperary—where many went to
In those olden days.

Whoever it was
Sat on an upturned tin
And smoked a pipe. Spring
Months were finished beyond the parapet
And winter not yet willing
To let him through the mist
Of that long valley he would try to cross—
While the earth shook from gnat-bites of gunfire
As if to shrug all men forever off its back.

He spread the map across his knees
And a bloated fly dropped there
As if its feet were made of fur
Or soot,
And crawled over villages he hoped to see
Easier than half a million men did.

With bemused eyes he followed it
In a moment of mercy and curiosity
To find at which point it would stop

And finally take off from,
Telling himself that place would be
Where the cloth of agony might fall on him.

His hand refused to follow up these thoughts,
And squashed the fly that decorates his map—
Pinned on my peaceful study wall
After fifty years gone by.

When night came he lit one of the lanterns
By which to count his men into the trench,
And crouching on the last day of June
In the deep earth slit that stank
Of soil and Woodbines, cordite and bitter shit,
He held the green wick close to his exhausted face
Which mirrored the failing marrow of his life—
Then shut the light into the safety of its case,
And ceased to think.

Alchemist

Lead melts. If I saw lead, I melted it,
Poured it into sand and made shapes.
I melted all I'd got, even my own, eventually.

I watched that lead soldier's rifle wilt
In an old tin-can on a gas flame
Caught like a straw going down
From an invisible spark of summer.
He stood to attention in the tin
Rim gripped by fanatic pliers
That believed in life and nothing else—
From the old man's tool-kit
Looked on by beady scientific eyes
That vandalised a leaden grenadier.

The head sagged, sweating under a greater
Heat than Waterloo or Alma.
With tired feet he leaned against the side
And lost an arm where no black grapeshot came.
His useless knees gave way,
A pool half spreading to his once proud groin,
Waist and busby falling in, as sentry-go
At such an India became too hard,
And he lay down without pillow or blanket
Never to get up and see home again.

Another one. Two more. I threw them in
And these went quicker, an elegant patrol
Dissolving in that infernal pit.
My eyes watered from the heat and fumes of painted
Soldiers melting under their own smoke,

The fire with me, hands hard at the plier-grip
Eyes cool but squinting
At these soldiers rendered
To a patch of peaceful lead
At the bottom of a tin.

Swords into ploughshares:
With the gas turned off I wondered
What to do with so much marvellous
Dead lead that hardened
As I looked, and looked,
And looked at it.

Synagogue in Prague 1963

The Germans said, before they killed:
'Death is the way to Freedom,'
But seventy-seven thousand names
Carved into these great walls
Make a prison that no death can open.

Legs walk, fingers touch,
Eyelids close in awe and sorrow:
That name was my mother
That boy starved to death, my son
Those men gassed—my brothers
Those who died of typhus,
Who were shot, stifled, burned,
Are my oppressed and swarming cousins.

It might have been me, and if it was me,
Where is my name?
I spend
All day there searching the words
Looking for my name.
I'd be glad it was not me
If they could look again at the sky,
Reach that far-off river
And swim freely in it.

What can one say
That was not screamed at the time?
Shouting rots the brain.
The dead God hanging in
His christian churches, whose followers

Through centuries have kept it going,
Will never hear—
Yet such Man's work calls for revenge
To ease the pain of having let it happen,
To stop it being planned again.

Huge crimson letters of revenge
Daubed on such a wall
Would be a vandalising of that mute synagogue,
And the seventy-seven thousand names
So stonily indented
Would still show through.

Vengeance is Jehovah's own:
To prove He's not abandoned us
He gave the gift of memory,
Which we must meet with our remembrance
In the land of Israel.

Irkutsk 1963

In Irkutsk a swastika was scrawled
On a wall so I took my handkerchief
And spat and rubbed
But it was tough Russian chalk
Wondering: Why those drab-faced bastards
Didn't rub it off?

I'd done the same in London
And here it was ineradicable Russian chalk
When I chafed it to the barest shadow
(No one taking notice on their walk
Down Karl Marx Street)
I strolled away muttering: 'Fuck it!'—
If they want it let them have it.

Apart from scraping out a concave mark
The crippled cross would stay forever,
And anyway why should I pay
For damaging the People's Property?

Zodiac Fish

I am a fish—so says the Zodiac—
and sit by a lake in Northern Italy;
but I was born in frosty Nottingham
and almost perished as a small pink squalling
dolphin-ball of flesh
turning blue in protest
at the frozen anti-fish world
of the bleak outside;
surviving when the fish-god drew my life-breath
into a mellower spring
that a weakling fish could live in.

I am a fish
so move like one in water,
an air-fish breathing the air-water
of land between earth and sky.

Like a fish in water—
I mix with people and am one of them
a grain of the great mass-crowd
of human minnows who don't know where they
     came from
and won't know where they're going
till they get there.

I am a fish,
but there are many kinds
in the zodiac aquariums of the crowded
universe;
all fish are in me
just as I am in all fish
and all kinds of fish are part of me;

I slide easily, but swim and breathe
with difficulty, moving
in the shallows like an oiled shadow
occasionally gaudy in my coat of scales
sometimes as grey as life
shifting to find food and ease of living.

Being many fish
I can hang on like an octopus
when some strong current sweeps me
to where no lithe and feeling fish
would want to go—

but I edge some way towards it
to find out where it is,
make sure and treble sure
I do not want to go there
because on first and second thoughts
I wasn't sure;

I am a whale
when the space to get me to a certain place
is opened wide enough to draw me through,
I am the biggest whale because
I won't be pushed by any force
to where I know I do not want to go;

but I am a minnow
when I need to flow beyond my pale
to green pastures and easy reed-banks
and the bottleneck's too narrow
for a normal fish to thread :
I turn into a green and tiny minnow
so small not even the slit of a gate can stop me.

Once through
or not through (a fish
will never say whether
he is where he wants to be or not
or even if he ever wants to get there)
I will stay where I am
and fight for my watery shadow-ground
and feeding-patch
if those who fancy themselves
as predators or fishermen
think to take me from it—

I become a shark in that case—
with a mountainside of teeth
rows of white knife-tips,
longer than any whale
more tenacious than any octopus
more shifting than any minnow,
one fish in its own spinning shoal—

the only fish left
in the world
who colours the universe red
and blots out the stars and sun
before the planets fly in
and break him into the pieces
of a final sleep,
which was what he wanted anyway
as he slides and shrinks
to a transparent minnow
and takes his last sleep
under the warm mud that,
at one nudge of the earth's shoulder,
will turn again into finer liquid

and set him free
make him one and only and whole
to roam the oceans
like a fish in water
with heaven in his mouth
and eternity at the tips of each fin
that guide him to a point of vanishing:
he stays a molecule of colour
that only other fish can see
when the sun shines
through water
from Como to Zodiac.

A Few Lines on Malvern Abbey

Malvern Abbey in the early light
Is like a toy that's grown up in the night—
A pretty, pinnacled and grey concoction
Carved out of sky and solid mushroom.
I stand level with it, at the hotel next door
Looking over the plain at the same
Long latitudinal cloud furrows
Of threatening rain that smell like snow to shepherds
Yet are good for the earth. God was always
Like that, the raw God called nature
Who rolled those clouds along and,
With his little men and women,
Made that Abbey next door
In no more than a night to Him—
Set it there during some barbarian's
Long sleep, surprising him when he woke up
With briars in his armpits and yelled at both.

It's a grey day, and won't get much lighter:
The grey stone of Malvern glows like a light
In this daylight, when seen dimly from a long way off,
A darker grey in Malvern's green
When all the mauve-green pigback can be seen
By farmers on the rainlicked Cotswolds,
Or charcoal burners in the Woods of Dean.

Learning Hebrew

With coloured pens and pencils
And a child's alphabet book
I laboriously draw
Each Hebrew letter side by side
From right to left
And hook to foot.
The *laméd*, narrow at the top
And then quite wide,
Sets the steel pen deftly thickening
As it descends
And turns three bends
To make a black cascade of hair,
Halting at the vowel-stone
And stepping-point to one more letter.

A page of script comes up like music
Blessing life and the first blue of the sea,
Or the season's ripe fruit
And the act of eating bread:
They look like songs indeed
Each sign a newborn soul
Hewn out of flesh and rock
By hands that wanted God as well as beauty.

I'm slow to learn, except these letters
With their cloud-tail shapes
And whale-heads, arks and ships
In black, pure black, the black
Of the dark enormous sky from where they
        came,
Behind a wall of flesh and rock.

With their surety and law
Such utterable shapes of beauty
Make me illiterate once more,
And gives a pleasure to the eyes
That hurts the heart
As if the sky is bruising it.

If struck blind I'd go on drawing them
Seeing in my own engendered dark
The visionary boat of life which
Floats upon the black flood of myself
And stops that boulder bigger than the earth
From crushing me.

Man needs such help, though rarely says so.
Lost in this slow writing
I clutch at that letter like a walking stick
That sets me tapping
Into the *samech* cavern-mouth where,
Though afraid of sleep I curl up
By another phosphorescent letter
Asking if it's *alef* or *tav*
Beginning or end,
Or still the lit-up middle.

Dreams dissolve the certainty of what it was
Yet when the light comes back
The blind hand writes
Hebrew letters cut in my rock,
And painted by a child on the page:
For they are me,
And I am one of them but don't know which.

Poem Written on the Hereford Train

Don't write a poem
The reviewer said.
Tell a story.
You are good at that.
Write prose instead.

Bollocks, I said.
Drop dead.
Get screwed.
Blow yourself up.
Fly to the moon.
Perish.

How's that for a poem?

It doesn't rhyme, he said.